Since its early beginnings in 1896, the motor industry of Great Britain has played a major part in the industrial, social and economic development of the country.

In 1983 The British Motor Industry Heritage Trust was established to collect and conserve artifacts and records of those companies which over the years have come together to form the Rover Group.

This year saw the opening of the brand new Heritage Centre (BMIHC) in Gaydon, Warwickshire. Here, the Trust's impressive purpose-built museum houses over 200 motor vehicles – the largest collection of British motor cars on display in the world, supported by a unique document and photographic archive.

Working in support of the collection are an enthusiastic and dedicated team of specialists who work in a wide variety of departments. Here we meet just some of the people working together to tell the story of the tremendous impact that the motor industry has had on the knowledge, expertise and skills of Britain's workforce and motoring public.

FIONA TORDOFF

'... this is a brand new site — we don't even have a bag of nails from last time, so in a way it's a curator's dream...'

My introduction to the industry began when I left Leeds University to join the Rover Group. The graduate training programme required spending time in all departments of the company's operations. That even meant working on the production line — a ground-floor opportunity to see how the industry operated. Later I went on to work in training-design and personnel management.'

Fiona's experience in Rover Group provided her with sound experience in project management — a real asset in her present job.

'As curator I am responsible for the collection; exhibiting it to the public, conserving it and researching the artifacts and archives. We concentrate on the brand names or "marques" that define the Rover Group. There are about 40 different marques which include such famous names as Landrover, MG, Austin and Morris. We try to tell the story of the role of the industry in Britain by exhibiting the collection.'

That story is not simply confined to the display of vehicles.

'I am not obsessed with motor cars, but what really interests me is "the story behind the bonnet". Information about how long someone might have to have saved up to buy a particular car in say, 1920, is fascinating, and that sort of thing enhances the exhibition.'

The establishment of a major new national museum is a rare occurrence and as a member of the management team, Fiona has had to assume other responsibilities in addition to her role as curator.

'I recruit 'front of house' staff — the attendants, and organise their daily work. Writing their initial training brief and taking them through the training is important because they deal with the public all the time. I meet with them regularly to discuss how their work is going. I also deal with people from outside the museum. For example, tomorrow morning I will be talking to a designer about the exhibitions policy; later I'm meeting a representative from a company which manufactures touch-screen technology; and in the afternoon I will be discussing some artwork with a sponsor for one of our displays.'

Each day is busy and brings new challenges for Fiona, but as she explains, that's one of the attractions of her job.

'We are a small team here so when we see that something needs doing we just get on with it, which is very satisfying. Because we are a new establishment, a good deal of my work at present involves general management. I expect that to change as the museum develops. There's a lot to be done in terms of curatorship and in establishing museum standards. As Curator I am involved in shaping the exhibition policy and I am very aware that the standards we set now will be judged by others in the future.'

RECORDS ARCHIVIST

GILLIAN BARDSLEY

'... a good deal of an archivist's work involves making sure that information is organized and easily accessible — which puts the archivist at the very centre of museum work...'

After a postgraduate degree in anthropology, Gillian spent two years working at Capetown University in South Africa. On her return to England she went to work at Coventry Transport Museum.

'My job was to supervise the documentation, shelving and listing of the museum's archive material which was completely uncatalogued. I also became Information Officer for the museum — providing the public and various institutions with information about the collection.'

Ideal experience for Gillian's job at BMIHC as Records Archivist. Here the task is even more demanding.

'We house over four million engineering drawings, many millions of documents, specifications and vehicle production records as well as sales catalogues and technical manuals — a priceless record of the industry. Unless things are organized they can't be used properly. I have to respond to requests for information from the public, other institutions and other departments here in the museum, so it's no use having piles of records all over the place.'

Organizing this vast quantity of material is aided by a computerised database.

'The computer program we use was written specially for us by a software specialist. It works on two levels. The **Accessions Register** provides a record of everything that comes into the archive — a basic register which allows us to find things quickly. Then we **Catalogue** the material with a detailed description of each item.'

Responsibility for such a vast number of records is certainly a challenge and Gillian admits that some of the work can be quite wearing.

'The scale of the task here is so great that it could defeat you if you were to concentrate on one aspect for too long, so I divide my working week. I spend a few days in the archive store — physically sorting records, organizing them and putting them onto the shelves. Then later I work up here in the office, recording the information on the computer.'

Not all Gillian's work is based in the museum.

'Although the major part of my work is here, new archive material offered to the collection is provided mainly by the Rover Group, so I also visit other Rover sites to assess new material. We are now collecting certain records from 1983, which of course will be historically important in fifty or a hundred years time.'

Collecting and archiving this giant library of material is only one part of the archivist's work. Gillian has published papers and articles and written a book on her subject. She also works closely with the photographic archivist and with the education department to decide on suitable material for exhibitions. Researching, writing and interpreting the information is a fascinating process which contributes in large measure to the enjoyment of the visiting public.

'There's no point in researching and learning all this information if you don't share it, so here I have an opportunity to contribute ideas and be closely involved in producing the displays in the gallery. I also give lectures to interested groups outside the museum, which can be great fun, and attend conferences and seminars. All in all I enjoy the variety and challenge of my job.'

PHOTOGRAPHIC ARCHIVIST

KARAM RAM

'...the 20th century has been the century of the car, so resources like this will be really important in the telling of the story of Britain's role in the industry...'

Armed with a BTEC diploma in photographic studies, Karam started his working career with a long-established photographic company in Birmingham.

'The company specialized in industrial and architectural photography. As a hand-colour printer I worked with archives and photographic glass plates. Although I didn't know it at the time, the three years I spent there were perfect training for my present job.'

Karam was eager to move into creative photography, so he set up as a freelance photographer. With funding from the Race Relations Board and the Arts Council, he joined a three-week expedition to India. The results of his work there formed the basis of a very successful touring photographic exhibition. He undertook more varied freelance work, lectured on a part-time basis... and also did a Masters degree at Derby University. Then he saw an advertisement for the BMIHC.

'The museum wanted someone with exactly my experience to manage the photographic archive, and I could see immediately it was a job I would enjoy.'

'I have several responsibilities. Caring for and cataloguing the photographic material in the archive involves literally thousands of photographic glass plates — 99 per cent of which we haven't yet seen. That makes it really quite exciting because I'm constantly coming across fascinating images that not only say a great deal

TRAINEE VEHICLE RESTORER

about the motor cars — but also illustrate social and working conditions of the day.'

With thousands of photographic plates yet to be cleaned, recorded and moved from their old wood and paper boxes into purpose-built storage cabinets, Karam has a formidable task ahead of him. In addition to caring for the archive Karam keeps up a busy workload:

'On a daily basis I run the photographic loan service which involves sending out material to journalists and corresponding with them. Work for the centre includes producing new images for the archives which will be of interest to future generations, taking publicity shots for our publications, and producing prints for sale to the general public.'

Karam also works closely with Gillian Tordoff to gather material which will be presented in exhibition to the public.

'For me, this job draws together all the things I am interested in; the academic study of the photographic archive, the opportunity to do practical photography, and the chance to be involved in the planning and construction of exhibitions... the perfect job!'

ALEX MAGLIO

'*...I like the atmosphere of working in something that feels big and new and special...*'

had worked for about eight years as an operative in a flour mill but was made redundant. After a period out of work, I was offered a place at BMIHC on Employment Training.'

Now seven months into the twelve-month placement, Alex is enjoying working with motor vehicles.

'I was always interested in classic cars and restoring them, but I'd never had the opportunity to do it. I work with six other mechanics and restorers and I'm learning a completely new trade. Most of the training is on-the-job, supervised by the foreman, and I also attend day-release at college working towards a City & Guilds qualification. It's quite a big career change for me but the skills I'm learning should stand me in good stead later.'

Alex undertakes a variety of tasks in the process of restoring the vehicles.

'Preparing the cars for spraying involves rubbing them down, panel-beating and masking out areas. I've also been doing quite a lot of electric-arc and gas welding. Learning how to use the tools and carry out jobs safely is all part of the learning process.'

Alex admits that he has had to adapt to new circumstances.

'Going back to being a trainee and attending college takes a bit of getting used to. I'd like to continue working here after the twelve months is up but there's no guarantee of that. If not, then I will still have new skills which I can use elsewhere. I've had the chance to re-train in something I really enjoy doing, and it's also a great feeling to know you've had a hand in restoring something that will eventually be on show to the public.'

MUSEUM ATTENDANTS

SIMON NORTH

'...It can be fun talking to groups, and of course you have to gauge your audience...'

Simon North has long been involved with the practical restoration of motor vehicles.

'When I left school I did Youth Training in a local car dealership. I did a bit of everything — mechanics, bodywork and working in the store — which gave me all-round practical experience of working with cars. There was an old car that had been lying in the back of the garage for years and I was allowed to restore it.'

Simon immediately knew that he had found a career he wanted to follow and he went on to complete a two-year diploma course in vehicle restoration at Colchester Institute.

'During the course, I spent weekends and holidays restoring other peoples' vehicles, and later went into partnership in a vehicle restoration business.'

When the opportunity came up to join BMIHC, Simon found a very different outlet for his knowledge — and a very different working environment.

'I'd previously worked on my own most of the time, but now I work with the public all day long which is a real change. The visitors have different interests; some are casual visitors with a general interest in the museum, others are real motor car enthusiasts and we have a lot of school parties visiting.'

The attendants play an important role in enhancing the visitors enjoyment of the exhibitions.

'Some people have general questions about the museum and the vehicles, others are really interested in technical details which I can usually help with. There's a massive archive here and we have the opportunity to spend time looking at records so we can prepare for likely questions.'

Simon also helps to make the visit entertaining.

'In one display I dress up as an Edwardian driver and give a talk to groups of school-children and adults about motoring in the early part of the century. I have to adapt my presentation according to who I'm talking to: some visitors can't speak English but I usually manage to get the message across!'

Throughout the day Simon is also responsible for keeping the exhibits clean which often provides an opportunity for people to ask questions. Other tasks, for instance driving the shuttle bus, manning the pay-booths, and greeting people at the gate are shared with the team of six attendants.

MARTINE TRINICK

'... I don't mind what I turn my hand to because what I enjoy most about working here is the variety of tasks...'

'I used to work in an office as a secretary and although I enjoyed it, I prefer it here because every day is different. We help people to find their way around the museum and the various outdoor events and answer their questions.'

The attendants are often the first point of contact with the museum so they need to be friendly, approachable and enthusiastic. They can be called upon to carry out almost any task, so a flexible approach to their work is important, and not least, plenty of common sense.

'This weekend we had about 3000 visitors to the museum and two special events running in the outside areas, so there's plenty of activity. You have to be a good communicator and be pleasant with people. This is quite a big site so you may also have to deal with anything from lost children to directing people to the various exhibits.'

All the attendants at BMIHC receive a minimum of two weeks training which continues throughout their employment. Training apart, attendants also have to use their personality.

'When we drive the shuttle bus we do a running commentary about the museum and the surrounding area. It's a standard commentary but we try to make it fun by using our own words and varying the content according to what events are on. I speak German, Dutch and French — which I haven't had to use yet, but this is a job in which almost any previous experience of dealing with people is useful.'

ARCHAEOLOGY – MORE THAN SPADE WORK

The popular image of the archaeologist is of a rather eccentric person who spends most of their time digging in holes in the ground, looking for ancient bits of pottery, or emerging triumphant from a Pharaoh's tomb in the desert — rather a romantic image and the stuff of Hollywood films.

Excavation of archaeological sites and the academic study of artifacts is of course very much the work of the archaeologist, but today there is a growing emphasis on conserving our past and interpreting it to the public. Archaeologists are concerned with the study of human past through material remains. They need a broad knowledge of the whole field of archaeology but often specialize in a particular period, for example, pre-history, Roman or Medieval history. Many also specialize in particular objects of study; coins, sculpture etc.

Inevitably, excavation destroys the archaeological resource, but in recent years conservation policy has encouraged the use of the planning system in preserving historic buildings and buried remains. This means that today's archaeologists, whilst maintaining their traditional role in preserving the country's archaeological heritage, are also very much part of the commercial world.

ANN MARIE DICK

'*...as archaeologists we are concerned with protecting the archaeological heritage of the environment, because once it's gone we can't get it back...*'

'My introduction to archaeology was a week spent as a holiday conservation volunteer with the National Trust, working on Hadrian's Wall. I found I really enjoyed the work, the people and working outdoors. It was a complete change from my job as a silk-screen printer and I began to think seriously about training as an archaeologist.'

At 26 Ann successfully completed an A level, then went on to study for a degree in archaeology at the University of Newcastle.

'I really enjoyed the course, but I didn't realise how difficult it would be to actually find a job after university. My first job was as a volunteer excavation assistant on a training excavation in Poland for Durham University.'

Working as an excavation assistant provides valuable practical experience, but certainly demands a flexible approach – as Ann points out.

'You have to be prepared to live out of a suitcase and enjoy travelling around the country. Most jobs aren't advertised

ASSISTANT ARCHAEOLOGIST

either so it's very much a case of getting to know people, sending out your CV and generally keeping in contact with what's going on.'

Job security is not always a strong feature of archaeological work.

'After several years of practical experience of working on digs, I was employed by the Museum of London on an open-ended one-month contract. After working that way for two years I was made a permanent employee, then two weeks later I was made redundant!'

Ann joined Devon County Council Archaeological Service, first as a temporary employee. Here, as assistant archaeologist, her job is very different to excavation work.

'We maintain a computer database of the Sites & Monuments Register for Devon. There are almost fifty thousand sites of various sizes in the county. These can vary from the site of a finding of an axe head or coin, to sites of major archaeological importance; castle or hillfort and so on. Whatever the size, we record them in detail on the database and mark them on the county map.'

These records play an important part in the planning application process.

'Each week we receive lists of planning applications from district councils. We check the records and if the proposed site is of archaeological interest, we look at detailed plans of the development to decide if a more in-depth archaeological assessment is necessary. The assessments can have an important bearing on how a council determines a planning application'.

'We are not here to stop developments going ahead, although the department can recommend that if it's felt necessary. But our main objective is to preserve the archaeology on-site and we seek to do that through co-operation. For instance, there was a farmhouse to be built at one end of a field which contained a prehistoric ritual site. This was picked up from our aerial photography which we routinely fly every summer. We were able to point this out to the owners and they agreed to build their house at the opposite end of the field, which satisfied everyone.'

Anne's work is not all office-based and she doesn't deal only with archaeologists.

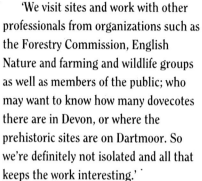

'We visit sites and work with other professionals from organizations such as the Forestry Commission, English Nature and farming and wildlife groups as well as members of the public; who may want to know how many dovecotes there are in Devon, or where the prehistoric sites are on Dartmoor. So we're definitely not isolated and all that keeps the work interesting.'

ARCHAEOLOGY – MORE THAN SPADE WORK

ARCHAEOLOGICAL CONSULTANT

Once it has been decided that an archaeological assessment is necessary, the developer is advised to seek the services of an archaeological consultant. These are the people who actually carry out a detailed on-site assessment and report the results to the County Archaeologist.

JULIAN RICHARDS

'...you could be faced with nothing at all, or a complex archaeological site, so you need to be able to understand the archaeology of a location very quickly...'

'Here at AC Archaeology, we are commissioned by a developer to carry out an investigation of a site. We work to a brief given to us by the County Archaeologist. Depending on the site this can be a fairly brief summary or a detailed specification on how they want us to proceed. First we have to assemble all the available data about the site and follow that with a site visit.'

It's particularly important for Julian to actually visit the site to enable him to assess the complexity of the operation.

'Some of the sites are comparatively easy to work on — it could be in the middle of a green field with easy access. The trouble is that initial plans don't always show land contours, so what might look like a flat field could equally turn out to be the side of a hill! Other sites may be located in the middle of a town and in that case we have to consider the difficulties of re-routing traffic and digging up roads and so on.'

ARCHAEOLOGY – MORE THAN SPADE WORK

In addition to specialist knowledge, the archaeologist requires a range of practical skills to carry out this sort of work.

'We have to mark out the site where we propose to dig trenches, and depending on where it is, we may require aerial photographs or a geophysical ground-scan to locate pits. We use theodolites to survey the area, so basic surveying skills are needed. All of us are fairly competent photographers and experienced in technical draftsmanship because we need to be able to turn site plans into finished drawings.'

The general public are often interested in the archaeologists work — which requires tactful dealing.

'Naturally people are interested in what we are doing. Sometimes they assume that you are the first wave of a development process so you have to be able to answer their concerns whilst keeping client confidentiality.'

Initially, heavy machinery may be used to excavate trenches before the excavation assistants set to work with hand-tools.

'Once the ground is opened up, you could be faced with nothing at all, or a complex archaeological site with objects that need to be cleaned, recorded in great detail and photographed. These sort of finds may also have a bearing on how you proceed with the excavation.'

The results of the assessment are delivered as a detailed report to the client who will forward this to the County Archaeologist to make a recommendation to the planning committee. It's important that the work is done quickly and to a high standard.

'Some of the work can be really tedious; we also carry out Observation and Recording. This is done for instance when pipelines are being laid. One of our team has to be on-site to record finds as the contractor is digging and laying pipeline. There may be nothing to do for hours but you still need to be there to monitor the digging. An archaeologist's life is not always glamorous!'

Julian explains that when recruiting new staff, AC Archaeology look for more than academic ability.

'We look for people who are enthusiastic and flexible in their approach. Most people do have a degree in archaeology or a related history subject, but that's not essential if they have practical experience of excavation and site recording. We may be running four or five sites over a wide area, so a driving licence is absolutely essential. Of course anyone contemplating this work as a career must be prepared to work outside, often in unpleasant weather.'

ARCHAEOLOGICAL ILLUSTRATOR

ANNE LINGE

'...in archaeological illustration we never talk about sketching! Everything we do has to be accurately measured and detailed, though you do require an artistic eye to make an object interesting...'

At university I read Ancient Mediterranean Studies and I had done A level art at school, but archaeological illustration was not something I had considered as a career. Later, working as an excavation assistant, I was often given the job of drawing plans of the dig and my career developed from there.'

At Bristol Museum, Ann works as a member of the archaeological unit.

'Here the team carry out archaeological assessments of sites for which a planning application has been made. My job divides into two main areas. I make the detailed drawings of excavations which are used to illustrate the unit's reports, and I draw illustrations of objects and artifacts that are found on-site. These are also published in leaflets, booklets and journals and are used to illustrate displays and exhibitions in the museum's galleries.'

Ann's work forms a permanent record of plans and artifacts, so the materials she works with are chosen to last: 'We use polyester drafting film, permanent ink and technical drawing pens of different fine-point sizes to create the detail.'

All archaeological illustrator's work is drawn to scale.

'The archaeologist on-site will measure the excavation and make drawings which show the plan, elevation and cross-section of the excavation. These drawings show features such as buildings, pits, ovens etc. I scale this down and produce finished drawings which will be used in the excavation report. Once the report is published, the plans I have made will be archived separately as a permanent record of the site.'

Even more intricate are the drawings that Ann makes of objects found in excavations.

'I receive objects of various material — bone, metal, pottery etc. Fairly complete pots are often just a bag of broken pieces when I receive them so first I have to re-construct them into something recognizable. This can mean gluing together pieces of pot to get a basic shape. Measurements can be difficult as I may only have a small section of the object to work with. Deciding the form and shape of an object also requires the ability to visualize it. That really can't be taught but comes with experience.'

Many of the drawings are scaled up to twice the size of the object so that the detail can be accurately shown. Later these are photographically reduced for the publication. Technique is important too.

'Archaeological illustration demands certain conventions. For example an object is always shown with the light coming in at 45 degrees from top left. Shading and hatching in various ways describe the material, so you use different pen strokes to indicate bone, stone and so on. All the drawings are made in black ink, but we use a key to denote the colours of areas.'

Like the plans, objects are drawn in plan, elevation and cross-section to show the complete structure of the object. Completing the decorative surface detail can sometimes be done by carefully tracing over the patterns using the polyester film and fine point pens. Later, detailed work with the pen brings the pattern to life.

'I work to deadlines so I have to be able to organize my workload and work quickly and accurately. This could be quite a solitary job, but as a member of the archaeological team I have plenty of contact with other specialists. I also have the opportunity to go out on-site and occasionally do some digging so I'm still in touch with excavation work.'

OTHER JOBS IN ARCHAEOLOGY

County or City Archaeologists, employed by local authorities, are responsible for giving advice on the conservation of sites. They often lead small units of staff responsible for monitoring planning applications and maintaining the county Sites & Monuments Register; a database of all reported archaeological landscapes, sites and finds in an area.

Archaeological Units are often attached to local authority planning, leisure or museum departments. Units usually consist of a small core of permanent **Assistant Archaeologists** or **Field Officers** with others employed on temporary contracts to work on excavations and other projects. A **Director** has responsibility for managing the unit, securing and allocating funding and overseeing matters of policy, especially implications of planning.

A growing number of self-employed **Archaeological Consultants** work on a contract basis for developers, industry, public utilities and local and national agencies.

In museums, archaeologists hold positions as **Keepers** or **Assistant Keepers**. The nature of their job depends on the type of museum they work in, but they are usually concerned with the curation, interpretation and research of artifacts. **Conservators** employed in museums and other archaeological units are concerned with the long-term preservation of finds.

Universities and some higher education establishments offer careers as **Lecturers** or **Technicians**. Universities provide some of the most interesting and progressive research projects, and some foster specialised aspects; for example maritime or industrial archaeology.

Inspectors of Ancient Monuments; employed by English Heritage, CADW and Historic Scotland, deal with the preservaton of sites and monuments, monitor fieldwork projects and recommend grant aid. **Historic Building Inspectors**; carry out a similar role in relation to buildings and have detailed knowledge of art history.

Those interested in archaeology as a career must understand that competition for jobs at all levels is fierce and there are many more applicants than jobs. Career progress often means being prepared to move to other areas. (see also **Employers**, page 24).

ENTRY & TRAINING

Although some non-graduates make a career in archaeology, realistically a degree is the minimum qualification and the higher posts usually require a doctorate or equivalent level of achievement. In museums, Keepers also require a museum's qualification, gained through the Museum Training Institute. A number of postgraduate courses exist for those who want to become involved in archaeology after taking other degrees.

Archaeology as a degree course is very popular and entry requirements reflect this: 5 GCSEs/S grades (A-C/1-3) plus 3 A levels/4 H grades.

Illustrators and other technical specialists may either have a degree or vocational training; NVQs/SVQs are currently being developed.

Practical experience can be almost as important as academic qualifications. Local archaeological societies exist in most areas and the Young Archaeologists Club is a national organisation for young people aged 9 to 18. Voluntary work through organisations such as the Council for British Archaeology and the National Trust can also provide a valuable insight into aspects of archaeological work.

ANTIQUE FURNITURE RESTORER

Restoring antique items to their former glory requires great practical skill and an appreciation of the originator's workmanship.

TONY VERNON

'...you try to do as little as possible to an antique, but in reality that often means having to do much more...'

Tony Vernon has worked as a self-employed antique furniture restorer for the past fourteen years and there isn't much that Tony hasn't tackled during that time.

'Normally people come from a carpentry background and learn the business of restoration from a craftsman. I spent several years in the production department of a theatre company where I learned the basic craft skills.'

Later, employed by a firm of ecclesiastical joiners and carvers, Tony's taste for fine craftsmanship began to develop. He learned the trade — restoring woodwork in churches and architectural joinery — from the older craftsmen. The work had to be of a very high standard and he spent four years learning the techniques of restoration.

Redundancy gave Tony the opportunity to set up his own business — never an easy option.

'I had always worked at home restoring items that people brought me.

At first I wasn't sure whether turning a hobby into a business was a good idea, but in the end I took the plunge. It took me about three years to establish a reputation for the work — but I now have a waiting list of customers.'

Tony's work arrives in his small workshop from private individuals, auction houses, dealers and museums. Some items are highly valued but Tony takes the same care with all pieces.

'I restore anything from grandfather clocks to cigar boxes, or I can make a copy of a table or set of chairs. As well as the woodwork, I quite often have to make brass hinges, locks and other decorative pieces, so the job requires a variety of skills.

'When restoring an item it's important to do as little as possible. This can make the work long and quite involved — for example, dismantling a chair leg just to fit in one small piece. The easy alternative would be to replace the whole leg, but that would defeat the object, so care and concentration are always needed.'

Tony carries out work on a variety of antique furniture rather than specialising in one particular period. This work can't be learned in a hurry. It calls for a wide knowledge of cabinet making, an ability to work intricate detail including marquetry and carving, and a gift for improvising techniques to achieve the desired results. Knowing how to use tools properly and keep them in good working condition is essential, as well as skill in mixing glues and stains.

Some customers have been very surprised at the results of his work:

'Someone brought me a set of what he thought were Victorian chairs. I removed the layers of dirt and varnish to reveal gilding and they turned out to date from 1720, making them worth about £6000 each! He was obviously pleasantly surprised, but paled a bit when he realised that his young children had been dancing over them for the past couple of years!'

Although being self-employed has obvious advantages, Tony points out that there is a downside.

'I work on my own which suits me, but it can be quite solitary. You also have to be well motivated and ideally keep to a regular working pattern, otherwise the temptation to take a day off could mean difficulties later when the bills arrive!'

Interest in Fine Art of all descriptions; from paintings and ceramics, to silver and furniture has grown in popularity in the past ten years. High-profile media coverage through specialist magazines and television programmes such as the Antiques Road Show has captured the imagination of the public… and encouraged more than a few people to search for that valuable piece in the attic! Once found, an item needs to be valued and perhaps sold. It's then we turn to the specialist Valuer & Auctioneer for guidance.

AUCTIONEER/VALUER

CHRISTOPHER HAMPTON

' The attraction of the business is that there is always something new to learn, and an opportunity to discover something you haven't come across before...'

'I started collecting porcelain figures at the age of ten. My father was also in the auction business and by the time I was thirteen I was helping him — unpacking tea-chests of goods and doing other odd jobs in the saleroom, so my training started very early'

Christopher is director of Phillips' Exeter branch. 'In addition to the management responsibilities here, my work splits into two parts; **Valuation** — for sale, insurance purposes or probate, and **Auctioneering** — which involves getting the very best price for an item in the saleroom.'

Christopher's job is anything but office-bound. 'We cover quite an extensive area of Devon and Cornwall. I spend a good deal of time visiting people in their homes and valuing items for them. It's therefore important to be able get on with a wide range of people from all backgrounds. The goods are as varied as the people who want to sell them; furniture, rugs, clocks, porcelain, pictures, silver and jewellery…, so you obviously need a thorough knowledge of a wide range of objects.'

On leaving school Christopher joined a local saleroom and spent seven years doing all the essential tasks — from sweeping up and making tea to eventually running a saleroom. The hard work paid off when he was offered a position with Phillips at their main offices in London.

'In this business there is no substitute for hands-on experience. Whether you join straight from school or at degree level, you are still likely to begin by doing the thousand and one jobs required in all salerooms. Later, some go on to specialise in a particular branch of the business, for instance, paintings or furniture, but it's important to underpin that specialisation with a knowledge of how the business works on a day-to-day basis.'

Phillips' Exeter office deal with more than thirty major sales a year. Putting together a collection for a sale requires a good deal of organisation.

'We plan a sale about two to three months in advance. Typically, it can involve as many as six hundred items. These have to be gathered together, stored, and photographed. Then we have to write individual descriptions of all the items for the sale catalogue. I do this together with other colleagues who are specialists in their fields. The catalogue has to be collated and discussed with the printers, and at the same time the sale has to be advertised.'

Christopher is assisted by a team of eight people which includes receptionists, porters, a saleroom manager and other valuers. The day of the sale is always a busy time.

'Our customers range from private individuals who might want to buy a particular item, to antiques dealers looking for stock. We have a viewing day, usually a Wednesday and sometimes a Sunday, and we often get families coming to view — so in that respect it's almost an extension of the leisure industry! From an auctioneers point of view it is something like being a teacher. People love to talk in the saleroom so you have to make sure you are heard and be clear about the bidding. It can be great fun and you can never predict the bidding, which makes for a feeling of anticipation. It's a great atmosphere to work in.'

It's also a job that requires flexibility.

'This really isn't a 9-5 job. You may be required to start early, work late to finish putting a catalogue together, and perhaps work some weekends. You need to be flexible, enjoy meeting people, and most of all be enthusiastic about the items you're handling.'

BRINGING HISTORY TO LIFE

The National Museums and Galleries on Merseyside (NMGM) was established by the Board of Trustees in 1986 to preserve and present to the public collections of national importance housed on Merseyside. The group is made up of six institutions: Walker Art Gallery, Lady Lever Art Gallery, Sudley, Liverpool Museum, Merseyside Maritime Museum and The Museum of Liverpool Life.
NMGM also administers the National Museum of HM Customs and Excise. The group is a centre for scholarship, conservation, education and entertainment, with an international reputation for excellence.
Throughout the group, specialists in a wide variety of disciplines are supported by enthusiastic support staff: administrators, technicians, visitor services personnel, museum attendants and cleaners — all working together to welcome more than a million visitors a year.
In this section we meet just some of the people in the Merseyside Maritime Museum who work together to bring history to life.

ASSISTANT CURATOR

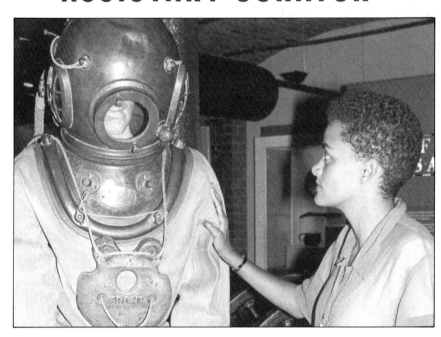

GAIL CAMERON

'...one of the more interesting parts of my job is researching the origins of objects...'

After completing a degree in English Literature, Gail Cameron's introduction to working in history was a three-year stint on an oral history project.

'The Merseyside Dockland History Project was largely a community project set up to retrieve information about the post-war communities who lived around the Liverpool docklands. It involved hundreds of hours of taped interviews with local residents about their lives and experiences and resulted in transcripts available for research, pamphlets and exhibition material for local museums'.

The project complete, Gail came to work at the Merseyside Maritime Museum as an assistant curator of Maritime History.

'As assistant curator I am responsible for the small maritime objects such as navigational instruments, crockery, uniforms and flags. One of the more interesting parts of my job is to undertake research on new pieces — to establish their origins and authenticity. For example, recently I was researching the origin of a cabin stove that supposedly came from the Mauritania. In the records office I was able to look at the original documentation of how the ship was built and details of suppliers and so on and find out which company manufactured that particular type of stove. In this case the information available didn't offer conclusive proof that this particular stove came from the ship, but the research process is very important to ensure that any item we display in the galleries is absolutely authentic.'

The open-plan office where Gail works is bright and airy, with views of the Albert Dock — a world away from the traditional image of the curator closeted away in a musty store surrounded by ancient artifacts! Computer technology plays an essential part in recording detail and keeping track of the many thousands of objects in the collection.

'There is a computerised database of all the items in the collection. I update the existing records and add details of new acquisitions as well as recording information in manual records for certain objects. There are also routine administration tasks to carry out and on a monthly basis I tour the gallery to make a note of the condition of the exhibits.'

Assisting in the production of exhibitions is also a task that Gail enjoys.

'We are preparing a new exhibition on Transatlantic Slavery and one of my tasks is picture research. This involves looking for relevant photographs, paintings and engravings. I look for as many sources as possible, investigate copyright, obtain initial reproduction rights and order copies of illustrations. The curator chooses which illustrations to use in the exhibition.'

Gail is also responsible for answering enquiries from the public and other institutions about the collection.

'I spend about a quarter of my time replying to questions about the collection. Other institutions may want to know if we have a particular item. Typical enquiries from the public involve queries about shipping companies that operated out of Liverpool and requests for information on certain ships.'

Gail is soon to change jobs within the department, a move which will offer her more opportunity for creative input to the exhibitions and involve writing exhibition labels for display in the gallery. She is clear about what she wants from her career.

'For the really ambitious, promotion means being prepared to move around the country to other institutions. I enjoy my job here and I want to continue doing the same sort of thing, eventually with more responsibility.'

EVENTS & PUBLIC PROGRAMMES OFFICER

JIM FORRESTER

'...I don't concentrate on 'numbers through the gate' — my concern is the quality of the experience once people are here. In the long run the reputation of the museum is what encourages people to visit...'

As a self-employed boat builder and restorer Jim Forrester might have had the perfect lifestyle.

'At Durham University I did a degree in English Literature and I was active in organising and stage-managing outdoor events and music festivals, but after leaving university I felt I also wanted to gain experience in a craft trade. I did a five-year apprenticeship in a boat-yard which specialised in building boats suitable for rivers and canals; traditional narrow boats, launches and small rowing skips.'

Later Jim bought a boat of his own, restored it, then travelled around the canal system repairing and restoring boats for clients in boat-yards and dry dock facilities.

'I started to do more and more work for museums — restoring boats for exhibitions. The Black Country Museum offered me the use of their boat-yard where I repaired my customers boats and in return demonstrated the craft to visitors. When the Merseyside Maritime Museum set up a shipkeeping department, I became Shipkeeper; looking after the collection of wooden boats.'

The post of Public Programmes Officer was created to manage and explore the needs of the 300,000 visitors who flock to the Maritime Museum exhibitions every year. With a Museum Diploma in Science and Technology and his varied career experience, Jim was equipped with just the skills needed for this challenging post.

'We spent a good deal of time looking at what the visitors wanted to get out of the exhibitions. Everything here is geared to education in one way or another, but entertainment also plays an important part in that process.'

Drawing up visitor programmes, recruiting staff and designing their training are all part of Jim's responsibilities. In addition, presenting lectures to the public and teaching makes for a busy and varied work schedule. In developing public programmes Jim works closely with marketing specialists and museum curators to encourage the widest possible community use of NMGMs facilities.

'We are keen that the Museum should also be a community resource. For example, Liverpool has quite a large Chinese community, so we would be happy to provide space for them to showcase their cultural activities such as Chinese New Year celebrations.'

Providing this 'living link' is also offered to a wider audience. In recent years Merseyside has played host to a variety of major events of national and

ROLE-PLAY DEMONSTRATORS

The Merseyside Maritime Museum Character Company are a highly-skilled, full-time resident company with an excellent reputation.

Throughout the country, heritage sites employ demonstrators (sometimes known as interpreters) to enhance their exhibitions. Most are employed on a temporary or seasonal basis. A formal drama training is not necessary, though many demonstrators do arrive via that route. More important is an approachable nature, an engaging personality and the ability to listen and respond in character to the visitor.

Training is normally site-specific with employers.

international importance. Jim acts as the museum's co-ordinator for these events.

'Over the last year Liverpool has hosted the visit of the Tall Ships and the Commemoration of the Battle of the Atlantic. I co-ordinate the various departments and outside agencies involved in such a programme. I attend meetings of the main organising committees, brief individual departments and deal with various aspects of the logistics — for example making arrangements to cope with hundreds of thousands of visitors. I am involved in securing the funding for our part in the event, recruiting the people, signing up legal documents, checking insurance, ensuring the publicity is right.... It all involves a great deal of

advanced planning.

'Much of my job is about communication with people and ensuring quality standards. I spend only about 10% of my time in the office. Dealing with staff and motivating people to give of their best is vitally important.

'We are very proud of this museum and the quality of the visitor experience. It reflects on us all, because there is a huge team effort and everyone plays an important part in maintaining standards. On a personal level I have been a conservator, a curator and an educator. In this job I find great satisfaction in pulling those threads together to present the work to the public.'

ASSISTANT PUBLIC PROGRAMMES OFFICER

CAROL ROGERS

'...I am in 1854 at 10.30, and 1912 at 12.30 — the variety is what makes my job so interesting...'

Working as a seasonal role-play demonstrator was just another temporary acting job for Carol. Little did she realise that three years on she would be responsible for much of the work of the role-players in the galleries of the Merseyside Maritime Museum.

'I did a degree in Performance Arts in Middlesex and went on to do several performance roles as an actor and later I worked with community and youth groups in Liverpool. After working here for the season, I was offered the opportunity to lead the resident role-play demonstrators — the Merseyside Maritime Museum Character Company.'

Carol is clear about the motivation of the Museum Character Company.

'Our role is to use our dramatic skills to enhance the visitor's experience. There is a misconception that museums are places in which everything is locked away in glass cases. We try to make the exhibitions accessible to people — bring them to life in a way that a static exhibition may not fulfill. We have two main performance areas in the Maritime Museum: the Emigration Gallery — which tells the story of people emigrating to America, and the Piermaster's House — which shows how people of the day would have lived and worked.'

'On a daily basis I am responsible for organising the resident company and the seasonal demonstrators. I start my day at 8.30am. The Museum is open to the public from 10.30 so the first two hours are given over to preparation and feedback. I meet with the role-play demonstrators and we discuss their roles and work on developing drama skills, or use the time for research. They then go on to the galleries where they perform as individuals. During the day I maintain the existing programmes with managerial and administrative support and training.'

Carol particularly enjoys the creative opportunities that her job offers.

'The most rewarding part of my job is the research and writing involved in creating a new piece. Here I'm provided with an opportunity to lift the story off the page and bring it to life through the Character Company. All our pieces have to be absolutely authentic so I work closely with curators and other specialists to ensure everything the role-play demonstrators do and say is accurate.

'We decided to produce a piece about Ellis Island — the first point of landing for immigrants to America in 19th Century. There was a great deal of information so limiting the length of the piece to twenty minutes, we chose to represent the medical selection procedure which all immigrants to America in that period went through. First, I spoke with the curator to find out as much as I could about the subject and then read about procedures and how people were treated and so on. I then set about writing the script, which features a medical inspector and three other characters from Ireland and Europe. I concentrated on the sort of difficulties that the immigrants would have encountered — medical problems and difficulties with language etc The visitors to the museum join in the role-play as immigrants, so they can experience something of what it was like to be an immigrant in that period.'

The Ellis Island dramatisation has now run for a year and Carol regularly reviews it's success by talking to members of the public and monitoring their response to questionnaires. In that way the approach is visitor-led. In fact, the idea for the Ellis Island piece actually came from a visitor.

As Assistant Public Programmes Officer, Carol is also involved in organising events. In addition, through her extensive contacts with local theatre companies, artists, musicians and sculptors, she is active in setting up workshop sessions for the public which explore social issues related to the exhibitions.

A final word from Carol:

'I really enjoy the working environment. Here, we are a department of interpretation which puts us right at the hub of Museum activity.'

EDUCATION OFFICER

DILYS HORWICH

'...you need to be able to work with a variety of people at different academic levels, and to organise and motivate students so that they get the most out of their Museum visit...'

Dilys read history at university and then became a teacher.

'I enjoyed it but felt that my promotion opportunities were limited. When the Merseyside Museum of Labour History opened in Liverpool, the post of assistant curator/education officer really appealed to me. In this job I became involved in the planning of exhibitions as well as in the development of the education programme. I later transferred to this post as Education Officer.'

More than 90,000 students from schools, colleges and higher education visit NMGMs institutions every year.

Dilys is responsible for planning and implementing educational programmes which complement the permanent galleries and temporary exhibitions that make up the Merseyside Maritime Museum collections.

'So many students visit here that it is not possible for me to teach them all directly. One of my main roles is to organise a programme of training sessions and workshops for teachers and pupils. I have about nine themes for in-service courses for teachers which link with National Curriculum themes.'

Dilys also works closely with the Museum's Character Company to develop role-play activities which support National Curriculum objectives. Working in this way releases Dilys to devise programmes for non-school groups.

'The museum is an educational establishment and our overall aim is to make the collection accessible to students whatever their age or ability. We cater for people from all backgrounds. It can mean devising a piece of drama for eight year olds, or an oral history session for senior citizens.'

As part of the programme for adults Dilys also organises a twenty-week series for the Workers Educational Association, and in conjunction with Liverpool University, arranges Saturday day-schools at the museum. Outside of the museum Dilys runs workshops for both qualified teachers and teachers in training, in liaison with teacher training institutions.

'I also write teachers guides to the galleries which form an information pack. These describe what's on offer and contain current information on the collections, so obviously involve some quite extensive research'

In addition to occasionally presenting lectures, Dilys recognises the value of the museum's human resources: 'Many of our curators are leading experts in their field so I look for opportunities to invite them to give lectures and present gallery talks in the museum.'

Proof-reading curator's exhibition notes, advising on the language level of labels in the galleries and producing archive packs which are sold in the museum shop, are other tasks that fill a busy and varied week for Dilys.

What qualities does an Education Officer need?

'You have to be self-sufficient, a good communicator and definitely well-organised as much of the work involves forward planning to meet deadlines. In a local authority museum, my workload would be contracted out, and I might not have as much outside contact with people as I do here. I consider myself lucky to work in a national museum with such a wide scope of activity.'

SCULPTURE CONSERVATOR

JOHN LARSON

'...conservation is taught in the classroom but the theory is not enough, you simply have to have practical experience...'

John Larson leads a small team of conservators who use their talents in the restoration of sculptures. Traditional conservation methods are used in conjunction with the very latest developments in technology.

'In the main studio we have installed heavy lifting gear which will raise up to five tons and can travel across the studio. This is necessary because we need to be able to manoeuvre heavy marble statues to gain access to them — sculptures are never in a convenient position to work on! Everything in the studio is as mobile as possible including the work stations... and the extractors as our work can produce a good deal of dust.'

Traditional techniques include the use of clay poultices and steam-cleaning to remove the black coat of pollution that covers many of the monuments in our cities. Small quantities of chemicals — biocides and bleaches — are also used to remove layers of dirt which build up over many years.

'In the dry process room we have a micro sandblaster system to clean objects. We work in a disciplined way, cleaning a small area at a time. This has been a standard technique for the past twenty years.'

In the laboratory above the studio, members of John's team use microscopes and fine tools to clean small objects and painted surfaces. Some of the work can be quite laborious. Working through a microscope on a painted surface can mean eight hours of concentrated effort just to clean one square centimetre. Patience is an essential quality for the conservator.

'A colleague has been working on the repair of this sarcophagus of Egyptian granite for about a year now. It was damaged during the blitz when a bomb fell directly onto the Liverpool Museum causing the sarcophagus to break into several fragments. The granite is hard and brittle. It is also heavy and fitting the pieces together was a major task. We work closely with the engineers in our technical services department and they were able to machine stainless steel dowel rods to join the pieces together. When this was completed we used a polyester resin to secure the fix, and the gaps were filled with coloured resin to provide an appropriate colour-matched aggregate.'

Postgraduate students are trained in the sculpture conservation department at NMGM.

'When employing someone within the field of conservation we look for a relevant background, in for example, sculpture. Training in conservation takes the form of an apprenticeship lasting three years. In the field of sculpture we work on a range of materials including ivory, brass, stone, marble, bronze and painted surfaces, but the learning process doesn't stop there. Conservation theory can be taught in the classroom, but practical experience is absolutely essential: I spend about sixty per cent of my time working with students on a one-to-one basis.'

Alot of sculpture conservation is on churches, cathedrals, municipal buildings and on garden sculpture. Consequently sculpture conservators often have to work high up on a scaffold in cold weather. They also work with other specialists; architects, builders, masons and professionals in the

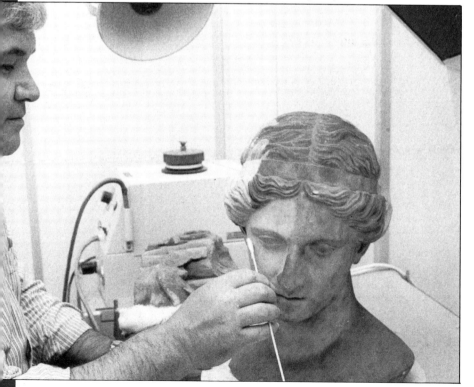

construction industry.

Scientists too are becoming more involved in conservation. Their input is increasingly important and John's team works closely with university departments to develop new processes and techniques. One such joint project is set to have a major impact on the conservators work.

'Many traditional techniques have associated problems. For example, chemicals used in the cleaning process can leave a residue which may cause long term damage to the surface of a sculpture; micro-sandblasting generates a great deal of dust and is a slow process which demands very careful work. In recent years we have been working together with Loughborough University to develop laser technology capable of carrying out this sort of work. We now have a prototype machine, developed to our own specifications which is the first of its kind in this country.'

John's work in sculpture conservation has earned him an international reputation and he makes an interesting point about the value of large-scale work experience outside of museums.

'Last year I was invited to travel to China to advise on the conservation of a huge collection of Buddhist rock carvings and sculpture. The problems there were on an enormous scale and required a good deal of logistical planning, recording of finds and site work. Previous experience of large-scale work is absolutely essential to tackle that sort of project.'

A National Centre for Museums Conservation is being developed by NMGM in a listed building in Liverpool. 'This new centre and the technological innovations we are developing here are very exciting. But in the end, it's important for us to remember that as conservators, we succeed when the public respond to the work of art rather than noticing how clean and well restored an object might be.'

CRAFT DEMONSTRATOR

DES NEWTON

'...it's important not only to demonstrate the techniques, but to talk about the history that surrounds the subject...'

At school Des Newton's favourite subjects were woodwork, metalwork and technical drawing — an ideal combination for the work he does today. Des learned the delicate craft of putting model ships in bottles at an early age — initially as a result of a challenge by fellow workmates.

'As a sixteen year old I was an apprentice welder in a shipyard in Barrow-in-Furness. I made models of ships in bottles as a hobby and to raise money for local charities. A workmate challenged me to make a model ship to fit in a light-bulb. At the time it was a challenge, but I succeeded and I've never looked back.'

Des continued his hobby through a varied career as a welder and later, as a successful entertainer. Eventually a move to Liverpool and membership of a model boat club gave Des an introduction to the then budding Maritime Museum.

'The curator invited me to demonstrate the craft of ship-bottling in the gallery. I divided my time between winter work in the restoration department — using my trade as a welder, and here in the summer demonstrating model making, until eventually this became a full-time position.'

The craft has a fascinating history.

'Originally seamen made ships-in-bottles and used them as a form of currency to barter for goods. Eventually the techniques became widely known so they lost their value in trading terms and over the years the craft has all but been lost. I taught myself how to do it by studying original models, so I'm using the same techniques that the sailors did all those years ago.'

Des works from a small workshop area in the gallery of the Museum where he demonstrates his craft to the public.

'I make basic models to demonstrate technique to the visitors, but for display models I am keen they should be authentic. This means I have to do quite a lot of research and work to accurate scale measurement to show the model exactly as the full size original would have appeared. I make a cardboard model to see how the finished piece will look. When I'm satisfied with that, I can go ahead and work on the finished version.'

It's this sort of attention to detail that has earned Des an international reputation and invitations to demonstrate his craft on behalf of the Museum as far afield as America and Taiwan. But the real secret of Des' success in the gallery is his irrepressible personality. Whether it's a party of school-children or adult visitors, Des' knowledge of his subject and ability to communicate his enthusiasm for the work, keeps the visitor enthralled.

'It's important not only to demonstrate the techniques, but to talk about the history that surrounds the subject; why the seamen made them, who they were and how they lived. That all helps to enhance the demonstration and encourages people to ask questions.'

ASSISTANT PRESS OFFICER

MARTIN LIPTROT

'...the function of our department is to promote the public's enjoyment of the collections...'

As part of his degree course placement Martin Liptrot worked as an editorial assistant for a London publisher; selling advertising space, arranging print runs and distribution and dealing with major retailers. After completing a degree in Industrial Psychology and further studies in personnel management, Martin also gained valuable experience working overseas:

'I spent a year in America. I worked as a barman in a bar in Greenwich Village, New York, and then later I worked for a photographer. My job was to organize photographic displays of his work in hotels, shopping malls and civic centres and to sell the photographs.'

Back in his home town of Liverpool, Martin took a temporary job with NMGM as a Role-Play Demonstrator on an eleven-week seasonal contract at the Merseyside Maritime Museum.

'That was followed by another temporary job in the press office. When my present post became available I was keen to be considered. Traditionally, press officers have a background in

journalism, but I had edited the student magazine at polytechnic and that, combined my work in publishing, in the 'states and as a demonstrator, was all relevant to the post.'

'The department's responsibility is to promote the public's enjoyment of the collections in the museums and galleries in the NMGM group. In the main, contact is with journalists in press, radio and television. We keep them advised of forthcoming exhibitions and events and we send them press releases and invitations to exhibition previews. This gives them plenty of opportunity to write about our activities.'

'Over the years our office has put in a lot of effort to make strong contacts with journalists, news editors and picture editors. When we contact them they know we'll have a newsworthy item and won't be wasting their time.'

Promoting a new exhibition requires an organised approach: 'There are a number of things to consider. We discuss the exhibition with the curator and decide on a strategy; who in the media we want to approach and how best to approach them, by press release, contact with a press officer, or direct contact with the curator. It's important too, to make sure that you are speaking to the right people in the media, and at the right time, so that the subject of the work will be properly interpreted.'

This is particularly true of television and radio.

'We might only have a ninety second slot on a news bulletin so we have to ensure it contains as much important information as possible. It's also very important to have everything ready on the day. We may have to stage certain pieces in order to achieve maximum coverage and ensure that the journalists are able to report the exhibition as fully as possible.'

The press office is the main point of contact with NMGM and Martin and his colleagues are very aware that they are representing the hard work of many people; curators, conservators, other specialists and museum staff. As Martin comments: 'It's vital that we play our part in bringing the result of all that effort to the attention of the media in order to reach the wider public.'

Martin's day-to-day schedule is anything but routine.

'Every day is different. For example, this morning I have been talking to a journalist about the underwater submersibles in the Albert Dock. This afternoon I'm discussing the John Moore's Exhibition — the largest and most prestigious open art competition in Europe. Variety really is the spice of this job. We work a basic 9 - 5 day, but we are on call for events, which might mean working in the evening or being available at weekends. Deadlines for press releases might mean working late, so you must have a flexible approach to the work.'

A press officer needs to be very well organized and an excellent communicator.

'As a member of the press office you get to work with a wide range of people; museum staff, who are specialists in their field and a variety of people outside.'

Martin makes an interesting point about working in a press office.

'I'd like to think that if I worked in the press office of a company which manufactured washers I'd be just as effective in my job. But I consider myself very fortunate to work here. We have such a wide range of exhibitions of national and international importance – there is always something positive to talk about.'

THE MUSEUM TRAINING INSTITUTE (MTI)

MTI was established in 1989 to provide a clear and coherent training and qualifications structure in museums, for the benefit of both employees and employers.

In order to do this, MTI is establishing a system of qualifications based on 'standards of occupational competence'. The qualifications are National and Scottish Vocational Qualifications, Levels 2-5, and all areas of museum work will be covered. The first two qualifications in 'Warding and Visitor Services' are available from Autumn 1993, and the conservation, curatorial, technical and management qualifications from Autumn 1994.

Many other organisations are also developing NVQ/SVQs which are relevant to the work of a museum (for instance in marketing, administration, design, photography, catering, retailing, publishing, security and archaeology), and further details of these can be obtained from MTI.

There are many courses which will help you to find work in museums, and MTI is establishing a database of long and short courses at all levels, from one-day practical workshops to postgraduate and professional qualifications. MTI can also send you other free careers information on receipt of an SAE.

**Museum Training Institute,
Kershaw House, 55 Well Street,
Little Germany, Bradford BD1 5PS**

ENTRY & TRAINING

Curator — concerned with collection management, research and scholarship. They specialise in a particular subject eg. Fine Art, Antiquities, Archaeology etc. and may also be known as 'Keepers'. Although in theory it is possible to enter the profession at curator grade G level with GCSE passes, it is extremely rare for non-graduates to be appointed.

Conservator — specialises in the preservation of a range of materials eg. paper, sculpture, textiles, metals etc. The usual route of entry for those with a first degree in Fine Art, History of Art or Natural Sciences is to complete a postgraduate course with practical training in a museum conservation department.

Fine Art Restorer — works in museums and art galleries, or in the private sector for dealers and collectors. They enter the profession in one of two ways: by becoming a trainee or apprentice in the studio of a competent restorer, or by completing an appropriate postgraduate degree. Competition for all forms of entry is fierce; very few apprentice places exist and formal courses take only a few students every year.

Archivist — the basic requirement for entry into the profession is a good honours degree followed by a one-year postgraduate diploma or MA in Archive Administration or Studies. Archivists work in central and local government, national museums, universities and libraries. Other employers include banks, businesses, charities, health authorities and learned institutions.

Archive Conservators — concerned with the practical problems of conserving archive material in its many forms. They combine technical expertise with an artists sensitivity to the materials they handle. Entry requires at least five GCSEs which must include English language, mathematics and chemistry. Applicants should also have an interest in a related craft subject; photography, graphic design, model making etc. Archivists and archive conservators are employed in central and local government, national museums, universities, libraries, banks, businesses, charities and health authorities.

Museum Education Officer — entry normally requires a degree or its equivalent, a teacher-training diploma or certificate, experience in formal education (either school or adult), and a proven interest in using museum facilities or previous volunteer work with them.

Administration & Organisation

Not everyone who works in the history 'industry' is an historian. The industry, in its many forms needs well-qualified people with good business, administration and communication skills. Those with BTEC/SCOTVEC qualifications and graduates of business studies courses or similar, are as likely to find employment in the industry as those with a history specialism. Conversely, a degree in history offers an excellent basis for further professional training; many history graduates go on to train as eg. accountancy or personnel specialists.

Museum Attendant — though formal qualifications are not normally required, attendant's do need common-sense and the ability to deal with the public. Training is employer led.

Craft restorers — normally train on-the-job with an employer to learn a craft trade eg. cabinet making, with attendance at college on day release and work toward NVQs/SVQs and BTEC/SCOTVEC certificates and diplomas. Further specialist training may depend on the employer. Short specialist courses organised by trade bodies are offered from time to time.

Valuers & Auctioneers — carry out

valuations and arrange sales of property. Property not only includes real property; land and standing structures, but also a range of moveable items; furniture, equipment, cattle, crops, and fine arts and chattels. Specialisms include **General Practice, Agricultural Practice, Plant & Machinery and Fine Arts and Chattles**. Training in the work-place is complemented with study for the Incorporated Society of Valuers (ISVA) examinations. Minimum entry requirements are 5 GCSEs (A-C) or equivalent, to include mathematics and English language. Three levels of examination, Part I, II and Final are normally completed within three to five years with part-time or full-time college attendance, or by distance learning. Certain BTEC/SCOTVEC HND/HNC courses and non-relevant degree subjects lead to exemptions. Success in final examinations is followed by a two-year period of professional assessment.

Teaching — can be a satisfying area of work for history graduates and one in which they can apply their subject in an interesting and valuable way. **Primary** and **secondary** school teaching demands Qualified Teacher Status (QTS). QTS is achieved in one of two ways; a B.Ed degree lasts 4 years with practical classroom training. Entry requirements are 3 GCSEs (A-C) or equivalent, including English language and maths, plus 2 A levels or equiv alent. Alternatively graduates take a one- year Certificate of Education (PGCE), which concentrates on professional teaching skills.

Teaching in **Further Education** does not always demand QTS, though applicants will be competing for posts with qualified teachers. In **Higher Education**, a higher degree is normally required; research is an important element of the work in this sector so academic qualifications are more important than teaching skills.

THE EMPLOYERS

Museums & Art Galleries

Over the last twenty years museums and art galleries have made themselves much more accessible. Nowadays the terms are much more broadly interpreted to include the heritage sector. The **large national museums** still offer the best route for the academic interested in pursuing their specialism. **Local authority museums** and **art galleries** include many small local establishments. Jobs in this sector tend to require organisational as well as re search skills. The **independent museums** and **galleries** that rely on sponsorship and/or the paying public, are the fastest growing group and these concerns tend to offer more opportunities for those with business and communication skills and experience. In all sectors there is fierce competition for jobs at all levels.

English Heritage is the largest independent organisation statutorily responsible for heritage conservation in the country. Its main role is to protect, and encourage people to understand and enjoy the historic environment. A permanent staff of about 1600, include curators, archaeologists, and other conservation professionals. A further 700 are custodians and maintenance workers. Quite often staff are recruited as Administrative Officers and promoted internally. Entry requirements at this level are a minimum of 5 GCSEs including English Language. Vacancies for attendants at monuments do not require formal qualifications, though experience in dealing with the public is preferred. Entry requirements for professional posts in English Heritage vary with the job. In Scotland, **Historic Scotland**, and **Cadw** (Wales) carry out the same function and employ a variety of specialists and support staff.

The National Trust and National Trust for Scotland employs a small number of history specialists: Regional Historic Buildings Representatives, Archaeologists, Conservators; textile, paper, stone, paintings, pottery, ceramics and environmental monitoring and control.

Wider vacancies occur for those with business, administrative or communication skills.

The National Trust also works closely with volunteers, providing the option of unpaid work for many thousands of people. Volunteers of all ages help regularly in a hundred different ways, ranging from unskilled tasks to those requiring professional knowledge. Training is provided for volunteers who make a regular committment of at least one day a fortnight. Other volunteers opt for placements of up to a year. A separate volunteer programme offers residential working holidays with practical conservation tasks.

Other Employers

Local Authorities, the Forestry Commission, British Gas and a number of civil engineering, architectural and planning practices.